Little Watering Can

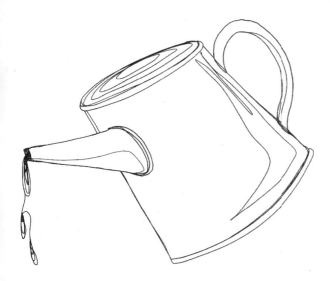

A book of when I fell to rock bottom

By Hayley Beattie

Illustrated by Vicky Carr

Little
Watering
Can

A book of when I fell to rock bottom

To Carrie,

thank you so much

for supporting me,

it means so much

to me ♡

love from Hayley

~ ♡ OXOX

3

Hello, this is Hayley!
I need to give a huge trigger warning on this book. This book
speaks about difficult subjects
like suicide, selfharm and sexual assualt.
If you do not feel like you can handle reading about that right now
without it negatively
affecting you, please put this book down (for now).

I wanted to create this book to show the people who are feeling
low, that they are not alone.
We are stronger than we believe
and we *can* get through this.
Thank you for buying this book
and helping me believe in myself.
I hope you don't relate to most of this book but if you do,
please keep fighting.
This world is better with you in it.

I want to give a huge thanks to my partner Stefan and all of my
close friends. Especially Vicky and Matt for helping me create this
book. Thank you for putting up with me in my lowest times but
also for believing in me.
I wouldn't be here without you all.
Thank you, I love you.

And in the summer evenings;
I tell myself you didn't mean it.

Stop thinking about everything so much.

You're breaking your own heart.

Hey Brain!
I thought we were supposed to be
on the same team?

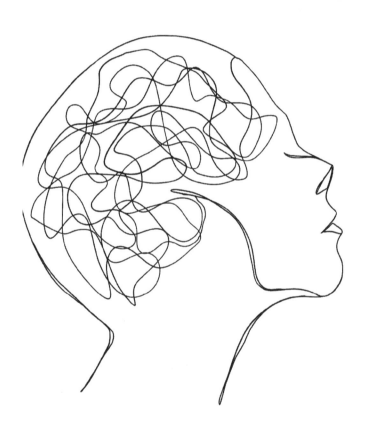

I want so badly to live
I want so badly to die
I dream of mountains
but I am dead inside

There's something awfully poetic about a tree being
struck down by lightning.
How could mother nature go against herself?
How could she destroy something which she knows is
beautiful?
Something that took years of nourishment and care?
How could she attack her own body?
I question this too when you hurt yourself.

We owe mother earth our lives.
We have to give back to her.

The darkness is like a smoke that slowly lingers and engulfs everything in sight

"<u>Reality</u>"

How do we truly know what is real?
If we perceive our dreams as reality whilst we
live them

Then... how do know we aren't in
one currently?

We daydream in the autumn afternoons
and
have nightmares in the stormy evenings.

When do we finally wake up?

Now that summer is arising
the scars you left me
are shining through
Oh how I wish it
would be winter again
Oh how I wish you
loved me too

I distance myself more and more
In an attempt to miss you less and less

But every video
every photo
Has me crawling back to you

I know that the ideas in my head
are the villains I write about,
The devils and ghouls
who could do only wrong
I know that they shouldn't be able
to persuade me

But baby they can.

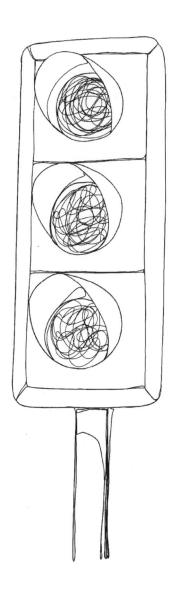

Don't hold my hand
I'm not in the mood
for looking both ways

How could you fucking do this to me?
It's so fucking damaging
Do you have no remorse?
Do you even remember what morals are?
Do you even remember me?

It broke your heart when he ignored you

How could you do the same to me?

I feel like rotting meat

the silence is so loud

I had so much love to give to you

But

...All you wanted to do was rip my heart out

I am writing letters you'll never read.

I only play songs that remind me of us.

And I wonder if you ever do the same?

...I pray I don't know the answer.

Being ignored hurts more
than anything else in the world
Why am I not enough for your attention?
I know that I repeat myself
but it's because
you didn't listen
or react the first time
I know my voice is somewhere in your brain
along with more intelligent sentences
that aren't mine
other seemingly more important souls
Am I not worth the effort?
Am I not worth the time?
Am I such a bother?
Should I cut myself off?
Would you miss me or forget me?
Is it worth the heartbreak?

Phoenix

Can I just die and be born again?
I just want to start over.

*As someone who needs so much validation
and*
reassurance

Please just

Say something.

*You felt like a ghost for so many years
and now that I have you; I can't seem to
let you breathe*

His arms; what a magical place to live in.

But magic comes at a price.

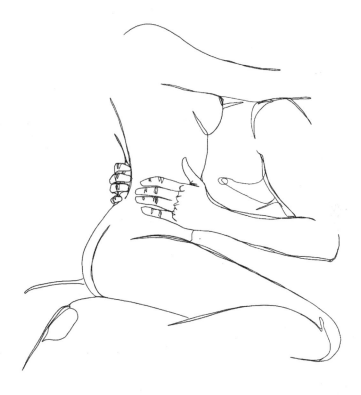

We're just friends he repeated

Just friends

It was completely destroyed but returned

- My heart when you left

I turn off every song that reminds me of you.
I am not ready.

Sometimes you just have to shut your mouth and let a person you love live in the happiness of the past.
A lie.
Is it unfair to break their heart for no real reason?

- heartbreaker

It's so hard to remain smiling whilst some-one is speaking to you. Especially, when your heart breaks at every word they say.

You're sweet

But

You're forever going to hurt me

The thing is people don't reach out

No matter how much they're hurting

That's why we always have to remind our
loved ones

That that's exactly what they are; loved.

*It's not right that I search for lyrics
to relate to
in break up songs
We were family
Please love me back*

It's strange;
Having to move on and let go

From someone who is still

Alive

Why am I not smart enough for you?
Is it because I am a woman?
Is it because your dad disregards
your mother's voice
as static noise?
Is it because you don't want me to
embarrass myself?
Am I really that unintelligent?
Are my remarks really that irrelevant
and ridiculous?
Would you like me to stop talking?

I have not hurt myself
I resisted the urges for so long
So tell me, why am I in so
much pain?

Things I have never told anyone:
He did not let me have the light on. Not at my house.
Not at his house, not in the bedroom, not in the kitchen, not anywhere. I still don't know why.
He did not let me cook, let me explain that a little bit.
At either of our houses; all I really ate was noodles. But I wasn't allowed to cook them. I was allowed to pour boiling water into my bowl of dry noodles. But I wasn't allowed to cook them. I don't know why.
Sometimes I wasn't allowed to eat at all. I would ask if we could go to the kitchen, to drink, to eat;
He'd walk straight out to the garden, he'd expect me to follow and my little deer legs would. He wanted to smoke. So we smoked. We didn't eat. I sat on his knee at all times, like a lap dog. I wasn't allowed to sit next to him. I wasn't allowed to sit near him. I HAD to be in his arms, he needed me in his arms, in his grip. No matter how uncomfortable, no matter how cramped. I don't know why. He took me to the gym, like the audience I was. He reminded me of his strength, he did that a lot. Hanging from things with one arm, holding me in one arm, lifting himself with one arm.
Restraining me with one arm. It wasn't impressive. It was scary. It was a warning. I took some photos with some male friends in college, one photo being me in the male friends arms, he didn't like that. I know why. He would hit me sometimes and in my Stockholm syndrome mind I said it was okay. I said that I liked it and he would do it again. I remember one time we were punching each other's clenched fists. I don't know why . but we smiled at how red our fists became. We took a photo, I don't know why. When I ended the relationship he beat me up multiple times, I guess he had a reason why.

It's been years; I thought I was okay this whole time. But now memories and trauma are flooding back and I don't know why. My housemate's boyfriend had the same shoes as you. He left them by the door, no problem. But I came downstairs; saw your shoes at the door and I panicked and I don't know why. After all these years I am happy without him, I am safer without him and now you know why.

I always crave attention and affection from the person who cares the least

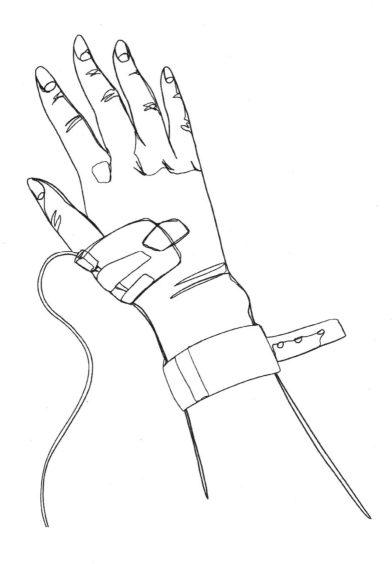

Would you talk to me if you found out I was in a hospital bed?

There's been so much fucking death in my life and it's only ever going to stop when I go under too.

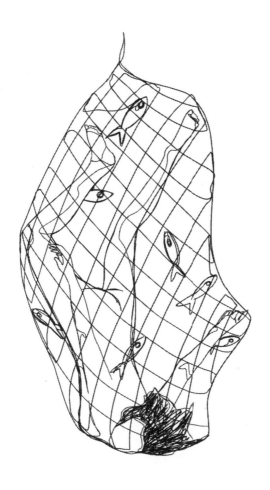

I DON'T LIKE LAYING ON MY BACK
MY CHEST FEELS SO CRUSHED
BREATHING IS A TASK
I FEEL LIKE I AM UNDERWATER
NO
I FEEL LIKE I AM DROWING IN SYRUP
MY LIMBS ARE ANCHORS
WHY DOES THE AIR SEEM SO THICK
WHEN WILL IT STOP?
WILL A FISHERMAN WHISK ME AWAY IN A NET OR WILL
I LAY HERE AND FOSSILIZE?
HOW LONG WILL IT BE UNTIL I KNOW THE ANSWER?

*I'm in a really bad place. Nothing feels real.
Everything is like a dream.
My body is weightless but my lungs are filled with
anchors. There is pain which doesn't exist.
It took me hours to get out of bed.
I am trying to cook but I feel so weird,
like I am going to fall asleep.
My body feels like it doesn't belong to me.
I don't remember things.
I am using cooking equipment but can't feel it.
I haven't been this bad in a long time.
The only thing keeping me here is the noise of the
knife hitting my chopping board
as I desperately chop these mushrooms
trying to stay grounded.*

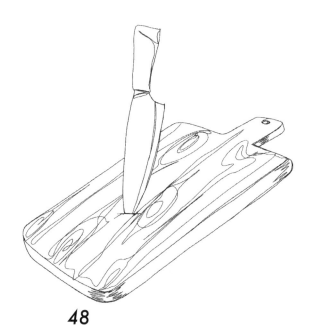

I feel like the inside of my body is
dark
my heart is made of wet coal
my veins run with lead
there are anchors attached to my
hands, feet and chest.

Poems I wrote in the hospital after
waking up from a coma
(high on medication) caused by a suicide attempt:

<u>Square people . . .</u>

If you draw 'people' and you put all your
care and effort into it; they would be drawn
as squares.

But if you 'rush' them they'll be drawn as Δ's
(triangles)

△   △   △△△△△   △   △   △△△
△   △   △

there are people that were squares (s) but
problems of life wore them down and turned
them into a real person.
I am a circle. O.

Poems I wrote in the hospital after
waking up from a coma
(high on medication) caused by a suicide
attempt:

Folding paper
You know when you fold
a bit of paper in half
by folding it, molding it over and by using
your thumb and fingers
and crease it?
If you do not concentrate;
you won't fold it properly.
You will not mold it properly.
If you try folding it again;
that fold will never be normal.
It can never be perfect
and will never be a 'great fold'.
It is too late.
You didn't concentrate
when you needed too.
Your old mark will always be there.
You've left your mark.

You live on in my dreams now.
Did you ever expect to find yourself there?

- I preferred you on the earth plane

I've always wanted to
save the world
But honey, I wish I could have
saved you.

I can't sleep when the world is crying
- nothing specific

I'm so passionate about
my mother earth
I want to save the world
and all of it's creatures
But I feel like I'm in this battle alone
Why does no one care?
Why are we such monsters?

Who am I?

Will I ever amount to anything?
Am I just surrounded by talented people?
Do I genuinely have any talents?
Do they feel this way?
Surely not.
What do I even want to do?
Who do I want to be?
Do I even know?
Have you forgotten who I am?
Did I ever know who I was?

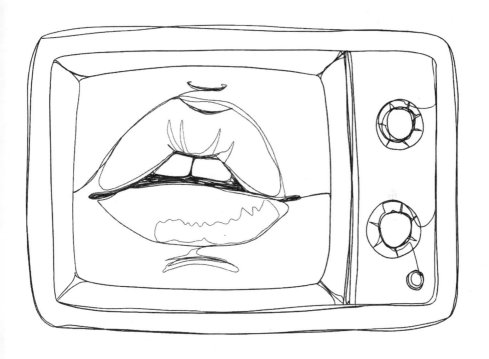

Does the sound of my voice sound like
the same news broadcast repeating
itself every 5 minutes?

WHY DOES EVERYONE JUST SEEM LIKE A RAPIST WAITING FOR AN OPPORTUNITY?

As I clung onto consciousness and
begged you

to CALL AN AMBULANCE

I heard you grunting; felt your body slam
against mine.

I let myself slip away.

It hurts when friends do things friends
aren't supposed to do.
Get your hands off me.
Stop feeding me that
boundary pushing poison.
I said no, didn't you hear me?
Or are my screams trapped
in bubbles
as I drown in your sheets?
What would you do if someone treated
your mother like this?
What would you do if someone treated
your mother like this?

So many women I know,
maybe all,
have a body engulfed in handprints
that they did not ask for.
Suffocating in the
"wow haven't you blossomed?!"
I just want us all to be able to breathe
again.

The Haunting

There are dark things inside me
Things I will never tell a soul
Secrets I will take to the grave
Like ghosts haunting me

Until I myself become one

The numb feelings of sadness seem
so welcoming

Like a memory foam mattress

It is easy to sink and remain there for so
long

Do I deserve to move?

Do I deserve to be hydrated?
To be fed?

Do I deserve to be awake?

Sometimes I'm not so sure.

An eating cold beans out of the can kinda sadness

When I was 6 years old
everyone in the entire
world seemed to be alive

Now however, it feels like
they are all 6ft under
and I'd like to join them

Sometimes the past is completely
unbelievable.
Is this why it's so easy to forgive you?

I wish that when I had inhaled my
first cigarette
I coughed my heart through my
teeth
And that I never touched them
again
But that didn't happen
I breathed it in
enjoyed the pain
And was in control
of my agony once again

-selfharm

Growing up and realising how many
men/friends/boyfriends
have actually assaulted you
or have taken advantage of you
is a truly terrifying thing.

Trash

I like Tuesdays
Tuesday is bin day
I can throw out all of my skeletons from
my closet

Dust the dust from my abandoned proj-
ects

However, I just wish I could throw my
body in with the other skeletons and
be tossed away to rot.

Being clean is such a dirty term

I am never clean

My mind is plagued with destructive thoughts

No matter how many months or years I go

without any harm to myself

The urges are always there

At the back of my mind

Like a crappy car salesman

Trying to sell me a stolen truck

You know it's a bad idea

But sometimes he just seems so convincing.

As if a stolen truck could get you somewhere

You know the place would be terrible

but it wouldn't be where you are now

Numb and lost

I'm suicidal
all the time
everyday, I just want it to end
but I can't put my family through that
again
I guess I'm just waiting for a bad driver
to deliver me to my grave

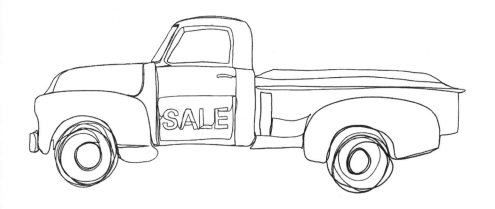

Do you ever feel so fucking low,
That you're convinced you have an
anchor attached to your tonsils?
A crushing-gravity-pulling-feeling
a grip at the back of your throat,
stealing your words.
People saying things like
"you'll be alright"
just seems fucking offensive.
Of course, one day things will be okay
but I'm really fucking hurting right now.
I think this really has broken
my soul a little bit.
My anger grinds my teeth
and my hearts sinks into cement.
I don't think I'll be the same after this.

*I have a flame in me which will burn
like hell until I leave this plane*

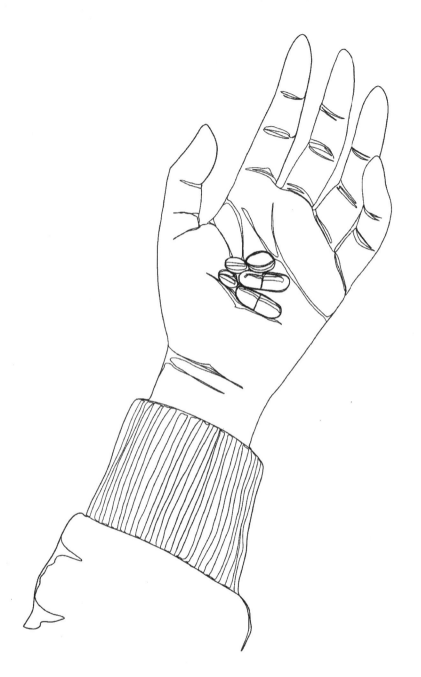

I am doing so much good with my life,
when will I stop wanting to kill myself?

The thought of you coming back
is cold and painful

...But it's all that I want

- You are like snow

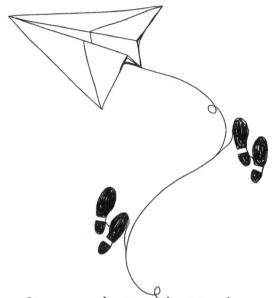

Since we last spoke I've been to six
different countries
Which is ironic because you were my world.

The worst part is
it all seems so out of my hands

I had a horrible dream
that you'd forgotten all about me,
I can't seem to wake up.

A death wish

When we were really young
We cried our eyes out
Confused about life and death
We promised each other
That if one of us died
We'd kill ourselves too
So that we could be together again
We sobbed for hours in each other's
arms
We promised

So tell me, am I dying alone tonight?

I wonder about you sometimes
Like how was your birthday?
Did you miss me?
Did you blow out the candles all by your-
self?
You had a whole cake for one
I bet that was nice
Did any songs remind you of me?
Did you do anything at all?

Since we last spoke
4 of my friends have died.
I missed your shoulder to cry on.

Being madly in love
Yet still feeling incredibly alone
is a very cruel sadness

Why are you crying again?
Have some self respect

Stand up TALL
They do not deserve your tears
You are worth so much more than this

I've grown so much
in the past three years
I've travelled to places
I never thought I would
I've lost so many
gained so much
And I've met people who have truly
changed my life
forever
I am blessed for the people I have met
I really do think I am getting better.

Today I decided that I was giving up
That I would crave you no more
That I would beg for you no more
I am my own person and this is my life
I was pathetic
I was at your mercy
But not anymore
I will live on, for myself
For my past self that died
begging for you
I am a new person
I am over you

There's nothing nicer than making a nest
out of pillows and stuffed animals
curling up under a blanket
and having the love of your life
stroking your hair
times like this make you believe it'll be alright

I am starting to not care about you.
I am starting to smile again.
I don't need you to
complete me
anymore.
I am so much stronger now.
I have such amazing friends
and insanely fun memories
even from when you broke me.
My friends showed me
that I do not need you.
They showed me how strong
I can truly be.
Maybe we'll meet again
some day
but for now,
I am happy
and I am whole.
Without you.

There's not many nice poems in this book
But there are SOME
And the fact that they exist
is all that matters
They are the moments I cherish

I wake up everyday

And I think, am I okay?

I can't really think any other way

I try to talk to you

But I can't really say

The simple word of hey

So I wake and there I lay

Not quite summer the middle of may

Is there a price I'll have to pay?

Please tell me you'll be able to stay?

But I'm coming out the truth is im ~~gay~~ suicidal

Life is so much more beautiful when you're in love

*My pelvis begs
for the warmth
of your hands*

My life is intoxicated with death.
My friends seem to be dropping like
flies
And my body aches for the same
demise

It's new years and

I've broken your heart again

After everything you did,
don't be nice to me.
I need to hate you.
Please don't make me laugh,
I need to hate you.
Please don't make me consider things;
I need to hate you.
Please don't be my friend,
I should hate you.
But now I hate myself,
because I don't hate you.

To myself,

I'm sorry.

Boys

Girls, when's the last time you cried?
Last night to your favourite show? I thought so
Boys, when's the last time you cried?
What?
Why are you looking at me like that?
I asked you the same question i asked the girls
You do know it's okay to cry right?
You have the right to cry

See boys aren't allowed to cry
Boys aren't allowed to be sad
Boys aren't allowed to be depressed
But boys are allowed to be mad?

See boys and mental health issues don't coincide?
Right?
That's not a real thing
A boy just needs to 'man up'

I've had so many male friends
Cry in my arms
Saying how alone and depressed they are
Of course this has only happened when they're drunk

Not in the day time
Not in a normal conversation
Only when it's 3am
They've had way too much to drink
And have nothing left to lose
As if being depressed is losing
Rather than a fight on it's own

No one chooses depression
No one chooses anxiety
Not girls
Not boys
Mental health affects everyone
And it's so so good that it's becoming less taboo
For the girls at least
But what about our boys?

In 2014
here in the uk - alone
4623 men took their own lives
That's 12 men every day
1 man every 2 hours

See i just attended my friends funeral
He killed himself
He was 19 years old
And in 3 weeks he would have been 20
But he didn't make it
He couldn't make it
He was smart
He had a future
He had a future

Continued onto next page

But boys aren't allowed to reach out
Boys play sports and boys start fights
When a boy turns to art
He's immediately a 'fag'
When a boy's passionate, he's a 'pussy'
When a man is crying
He's just a boy

As if emotions change your age
As if preferring art changes your sexuality

This can't go on
We cannot let this go on
There must be more people that care about this
There must be more people that feel that they're
allowed to cry

So please boys
Cry to me
Cry to me until you can't
Cry to me
Until your words run out
Cry to me
Until you need a glass of water
Cry to me
Until ~~you~~ we laugh

I'll be damned if I lose more friends this way

So just please cry to me,
I'll cry with you too.

An open window

Do you remember how we used to listen to stupid parody rap and smoke until the sun came up?
Do you remember when we'd cuddle because you left the window open and we were too lazy to close it?
Do you remember when we'd google pretty places nearby just to go and smoke there
Do you remember when we'd speak about our aspirations and future and how we'd never leave each other?

I do
But now I smoke all night alone to sad songs.
Now I am speechless.
I have nothing to say to anyone.
Now I go to those places alone and smoke until my lungs burn because at least then I'll be able to feel something.
Now I don't think about the future because it doesn't feel like there is one without you.
And I still leave the window open because I cant fucking breathe.

Why do I always seem to care
So much more than anyone else?

-dramatic

I guess I should be thankful

That I have the opportunity to miss

-To the good times

The Hard Part

Losing your bestfriend isn't the hard part
The hard part is that you are never ever going to see
them again
The hard part is trying to comprehend why
your chest is in physical pain
The hard part is that you see them happy in your
dreams
That is the hardest
as lovely as it seems
The hard part is wondering how they'd be now
The hard part is wondering why? and how?
The hard part is wondering if you'd still be friends
If this life hadn't taken the tragic end
The hard part is finding clips out of the blue
The hard part is wanting those clips to be new
The hard part is wondering if they're at peace
The hard part is that the hard parts seem to increase
The hard part is when someone has the audacity to tell
you to get over it
But your name will always linger in my spit
The hard part is that no one understands
And the hard part is that with hard parts I am damned
The hard part is that it's so much harder than it seems
but with all the hard parts
I'll still see you in my dreams,
I love you.

*I am starting to throw away things
you gave me*

*So I must be getting better
It's heartbreaking but I'm ready*

*To my lover who rubbed my back
whilst I laid on your bathroom floor
sobbing and dissociating
thank you for keeping me grounded*

I love you Stefan, and I'm sorry.

It's been 584 days but I'm not counting
Counting would scare you away
It's been one year seven months and 6 days
Please come back
It's been 1 year 7months of panic attacks
1 year 7months of rage attacks
1 year 7months of not knowing what to do
1 year 7months of how do I get through to you?
1 year 7months of blocked phone calls and
soaked pillows
1 year 7months of "I'm trying to be happy so I'm
wearing the colour yellow!"
1 year 7months of "WHY THE FUCK DON'T YOU
LOVE ME?"
1 year 7months of "don't you want to hug me?"
1 year 7months of "hey I didn't know you were a
twin!"
1 year 7months of "where the hell have you
been?"
1 year 7months where half of me I lack
1 year 7months, I'm tired please come back

My anxiety inside my depressed chest
is like a trapped bird trying to escape it's
cage
What would happen if I let it out?

My poetry might suck but it's my entire raw soul

I can't tell you about my
psychotic episode
because you won't be my friend
anymore.
So I'm sat here in my inappropriate panic
attack state
debating whether suicide
is a rational option

It shouldn't be normal that we put life
under taste
It shouldn't be normal that we have dead
bodies in our waste
It shouldn't be normal
The way calves cry out to their mother
It shouldn't be normal
That we don't love each other

- this isn't normal

We cut the water with our glass
Plague the sands with our plastics
Hang the birds with fishing wire
We are so much less than fantastic

Lately I've been so low that I can't write. I can't put my thoughts into words

But here I am putting my pen to paper

So I must be getting there?

- I hope

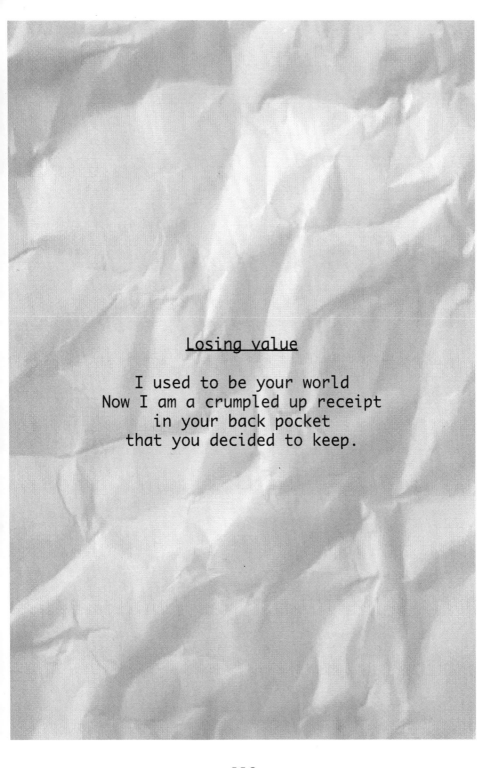

Losing value

I used to be your world
Now I am a crumpled up receipt
in your back pocket
that you decided to keep.

Some people are so kind;
The world does not deserve them.
I was so lucky to have known you.

-To Rajiv

They live on in your stories,
in your art,
in your memories,
your dreams,
in your heart,
they are all around us.
Like lyrics to your favourite songs;
their quotes play in your head like
verses of your favourite book.

-We have to carry on their stories

It's a shame that we seem to always live up to our saddest fears.

WAKE UP

I wouldn't have taken 47 tablets if I wanted to wake up
Please stop calling survivors attention seekers and wake up
This is an epidemic
Wake up
With crushed velvet wrists I will sign every petition against cutting funds to our NHS
The NHS who attempt to save children
from cutting themselves this is not something we can shy away from
Wake up
Children are not making it to their 20's
They truly believe that they are burdens
They're having panic attacks in their rooms
Whilst their parents are watching television unaware downstairs
Wake up
We have to change this
The generation below us cannot go through the pain we have
We can't allow it
We have to change the future
They are the future
so in turn,
We are the future
Wake up

My brain is a cross junction on a freeway
Except there are no red lights
No safety measures
Everything flies by and if it crashes then it crashes
And oh boy does it like to
My brain never stops
Every thought is bad
Sometimes however
Someone pours thick tar onto the intersection
Everything slows
Everything stops
I am numb
I cannot move
I cannot think
This carries on until so many cars build up that my brain
can't take it anymore
And everything is at once
The urges
The regrets
The pain
Whizzing by
This is when I dissociate
What did you just say?
I don't think I heard you
The cars were too loud
Why do I feel like my legs don't work?
My brain is just driving me place to place
Everything is so foggy
Must be the exhaust pipes
I hope one day my roads turn into paths
For people to walk down and wave hello to each other
For now I guess I just have to keep looking both ways
Until I find the lollipop man in me

I've lost a few people recently,
It's been devastating.
This year broke my heart in ways I didn't
know it could.
I was at the bottom of a well
and then I found a
trap
d
o
o
r

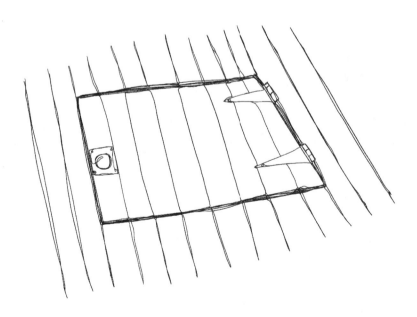

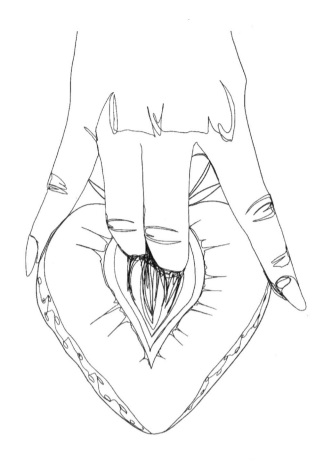

You are my summer fruit
Sweet and ripe
fresh and fragile
You are beautiful
As you blossom
You are good for me
But can be dessert too
Place yourself upon my tongue
For you are the best thing I've ever picked

- Growing up together

I am a bruised peach
I have been used
I will biodegrade
Into my mother earth

But not until I help fix her
One day flowers will bloom where I once laid
Please carry on the rebellion to help protect our
mother

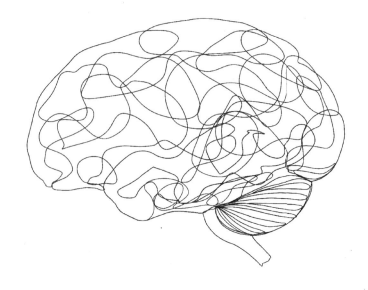

*I'll have a half depression - half rational
brain to go
with chocolate on top please*

Would you care about me
If I cared about you too?
Would you care about me
If I was the only person you knew?
Would you care about me
If you were me and I was you?
Would you care about me
If everything fell through?
Would you care about me
If my lips were turning blue?
Would you care about me
Is there anything i can do?
Would you care about me
Is there anyone else? If so, who?
Who can share this pain with me
Is there a queue?
Would you ever care about me?
Can we start afresh?
Start anew
Too ever see you smile again, that would be a
view
Would you ever care about me if I cared
about you?
I'm not just your enemy
I'm your sister too.

If I sigh hard enough
Will it lift this boulder
From my chest?

Losing a friend

I could never write a poem for what we had
It would never quite be good enough
And would be rather sad
Because what we had was special
And what we had was pure
And what we had was different
And that's what I adore
It all sounds rather romantic
For that I'm not so sure
See we were only young when we met
We were only four
But nothing I write will never be good enough
And nothing can ever cure
The hole in my heart
That just wasn't there before
See now I feel so lost
And like everything is so temporary
Like everything comes at a cost
But on the contrary
Some days last forever
The days when I'm feeling blue
I think of the days we played together
The days back with you
However this poem will never do justice
To the friendship we had
As this poem is just too painful to finish
And just rather sad.

Mercy

I want to be restrained
I want to be begging for your mercy
However,
what I don't want is our fishes to choke on our plastics
I don't want our fishes restrained in our wires and ropes
I don't want the ocean begging for our mercy.

And when I drink tea I only want a splash of almond milk
not a litre, ruining my day like oil to the oceans

And when I have a bath I want to soak in it
not drown
Like polars bears to our melting ice caps

And when I'm changing up my style, experimenting
know that I'm not a lab rat being forced into it

And when I cut my hair
know that it is out of nourishment and love
not a company begging for mother earth's forests to grow
faster

And if you have some eggs, why not have them poached?
Like every damn animal in the jungle and safari

And when you put on perfume, try not to choke the person
next to you
like CREEPY CRAWLIES drenched in pesticides

And when I go on a date,
I want things to be sweet, consensual
Unlike cows forcibly raped
just for their children to be taken away as if we had
ANY right

And if I take the bus
know that I still feel guilty
for the Co2 pumped into my mother earth's lungs

And when you go to sleep tonight
know that it's peaceful
and not forced unlike a pet on an ice cold table
due to inbreeding

And if you take a shot be thankful it's not through your
skull
because you FELL OVER during a horse race

So when you get that drink
PLEASE
just leave the straw behind and don't make mother
earth beg for our mercy.

I wish this house wasn't so dusty
I wouldn't cough as much
While I lie on crying on the floor
If I only had motivation to hoover
If only I had motivation to hoover
If only I'd turn to dust

I thought by the end of this book we'd be friends again
But life doesn't work out like that

Forgive yourself
We are all running through life
for the first time.
We can't possibly get it ALL right
the first time

I had gotten enough sleep
woken up early
I had eaten
and had been in the sun
all day
I was giddy
I had energy
I was laughing
I did not know this girl

I am trying to overcome the realisation
that I may never get better.

That I am plagued with mental illness for
the rest of my days
no matter how good my diet ,
my routine,
my doings.
I am trying to forgive my brain for this,
I am trying.
I know my body just wants me to be well.
I know my brain is trying
it's utmost hardest.
I know it is diseased and I don't know it.
I know we are two,
we have to be.
I want to forgive you,
I really do.

When I walked in on someone else
Holding back your hair
Whilst you vomited at a new years eve par-
ty,
That was when I knew that
I'd lost you

a half empty cot

The echo of your voice
Still whispers in the air
I am aching all over
My heart in utmost despair
I keep grabbing at my skin
It's so weird
To be in a world you are not within
I keep picking at my nails
The rainy days are now forever hail
We were sisters
Until the end
We were twins
You were my best friend
This poem sounds awfully a lot
As if you have died
Fortunately not
Though myself I've tried
I wish you would just answer the phone
They repeat and repeat
Endless dial tones...
This poem is so hard to write
I don't want this to be real
I promise I don't bite
But I just wish you knew how I feel
I dream about you a lot
I dream that we're friends again
We used to share the womb
then a cot
And we shared each other's pain

We used to play hand in hand
Now the ground is constant sinking sand
My mind is my enemy
There's only pictures of you
I am alone, I am one
But I used to be two

People often say my boyfriend is
not 'manly enough'
But that's who I fell in love with.
I fell in love with a pretty, artistic,
soft boy.
I fell in love with silly jokes and
flamboyant hand gestures.
I fell in love with poetic songs and
swing sets till dusk.
I fell in love
And that's more than enough

This is a poem
For the bad days
A poem for the days
You can't get out of bed
It's okay
Get some sleep
Maybe marathon a show
Don't blame yourself
For your silly brain
The sun will soon set
The stars will shine
As will you

*I throw myself so deeply
into every poem*

*Only the bottom of the ocean
knows my pain*

*All of the poems about you
sound like an ex love affair*

Oh how much easier that would have been

It's dangerous,
wanting to be controlled
You often end up in the hands
that don't deserve you

Do you have no self respect?
The words claw up my neck
How could you not want to be yourself?
Do you wish to be someone else?

My poetry is a scramble of words
that I have never had the confidence to
speak
when the time was right or necessary
An insecurity of a song is a mess
My mind is bled into paper
It's a release and even though it helps
I still don't know how to speak to anyone

You hide behind language barriers

And half closed doors

You are a coward

I hope your son never grows up
to become you

They say I wear my heart on my sleeve

That explains the blood

"Why do you always cling
to toxic people?"

The worst part is

I don't even hate him

Dragging a blade across your skin will
not fix anything

You are beautiful
You are/I am a canvas

But blood cannot be your/our watercolor

Christmas is on the way

The only day we voluntarily wake up way
before 10am

When an empty bottle of prosecco at noon
is normal

and there's a tree in the middle
of the living room

A day when we all love each other
wholeheartedly

and if we don't
we repeat

"Come on, it's Christmas"

A starry night sky painted in the colour orange.
A beautiful speckled with freckles face.
You are like autumn,
your leaves will fall away
and you will grow again.
- Chloe

I wish I knew that I could be gay
from an earlier age
Oh how many more lips I could have kissed

Lesbian Macoroni

A jumble of legs in the bed sheets
A separate pair of lips
come to meet
A strawberry and cherry fragrance
intertwining
A different,
a certain type of dining
Two sets of thrilled underwear
own the floor
A 'do not disturb' sign
hangs from the door

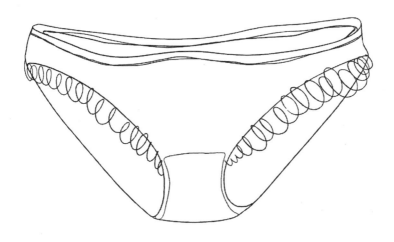

I've ticked so many things off
my bucket list
And you weren't there

I wanted to experience them together

I guess I'll just have to remember for
you.

I am plagued with the fact that I want to fix
the entire world
But I am afraid;
a small woman like myself;
cannot save you all
- Everything matters

If it was a choice
You'd think people wouldn't kill
themselves over it
- Gay

We are just two "snowflakes" trying to survive in the desert of today's society.

You are the embodiment of a sunset
Warm
Beautiful
Breathtaking
Now please go down

Seeing you sleep
watching your chest
rise and fall
one of the most precious
moments of them all

In these moments, this life thing
isn't all that bad.

Why do all the young
beautiful heartbreakers
have the same soul crushing cologne?

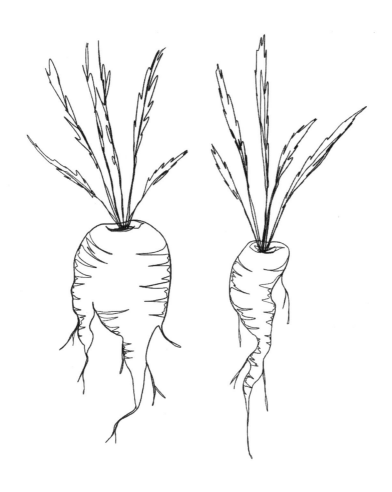

We are allowed to be a little different.
Even Lidl accepts wonky vegetables now.
So, maybe there's hope for us.

Am I valid now?
Am I valid now?

- Regrets

For over a decade
I have been convinced that
my life will end in suicide

...But it doesn't have to.

- A realisation

It was 2:12am when I sent you that text.
I was lying on the bathroom floor
having a meltdown.
I was lying on the floor when I decided I
would not
hurt myself.
I was lying on the floor
when I decided I would not end my life.

It was 2:26 when you came into
the bathroom.
You just came in to brush your teeth,
you hadn't seen the text.
You wondered why my 'quick shower'
had taken a while.

You laid on the floor with me
You hugged me
You took me to bed
I realised you were my life.

I love you more than
anything in the entire universe
And one day
I will love more people
Half you
Half I

The first time I realised I was poor
Was in - you guessed it- year 4
We were discussing whether a bath
or a shower
was more eco friendly
Everyone said shower,
I said bath.
Glances.
I explained how in my home;
3 people
would share the same bath water.
My sister and I together,
then my mum.
I didn't understand this,
to be disgusting.
I knew it as normal.
People looked at me strangely;
starting to realise maybe I was a little scruif-
fer than the rest of them.
I remember the teacher
trying to move on
as people whispered
I was an outcast now
I was dirty.

For the men beaten down
From woman who hide behind their
vaginas
The innocent face
Painting you in purple and blue
Break away from the unspoken
From the delicate hands which tie
ropes around your neck

Break away and don't look back

Our entire being can and does live in
their culture
-We are the same

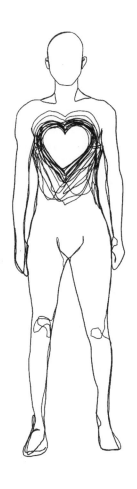

A male who can show his heart
Is a male where all men
should follow
An expressive male is a start
From years of ignorance
and repressed sorrow

Lost in paris
We breathe in the night air
Young students in their overdraft
Laughing without a care

Bags under our eyes
And knots in our hair
A love like this
seems so rare

I truly could be with you
anywhere

A fun little duo
An intoxicated pair

Never be afraid to love until it hurts

Drunk quotes from a female toilet at almost 2am

1.The world is not ready for next generation of woman!
2. If we get it right; we can change the world!
3. Girls toilets; they're the future!

I am sitting at a starbucks window
With an extra chocolatey hot chocolate
(with cream on the top!)
Whilst I wait for my true love to go on a
break
And I am so happy to say
I think I'm going to get better

I was blessed with you
by my true love
when I needed it the most
But I promise there is enough room
in my repairing heart
to truly love you too

I was sobbing in your arms
over problems you could not solve
You called me your "little watering can"
to try and make me smile
then I realised pain could bring life
pain can become art
this is a process
and if my pain could help anybody
bloom
then I am willing to take that sacrifice
and show my pain
~~I am~~ You are not alone

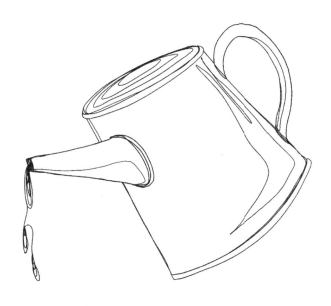

You hug me and pull me like
your childhood dolly
Tell me every last secret
Speak to me
I'm listening
You are so beautiful
Please keep taking me
everywhere you go
Please never let go

And after all these years;
how was I lucky enough to
be with you

I never knew how much love
I was capable of giving
until you came into my life.
I love you.

He doesn't know I use the soap he made me every night so that I go to sleep feeling loved by him

I don't want you to relate but I'm glad somebody empathises

*I inhaled toxic fumes because
they were decorated with your
name
A familiar fragrance which my
lungs would always welcome*

After feeling so much love by
the people around me
After so much validation
and reassurance
I think I'm gonna be okay
It's taken a lot of self love
It's taken a lot of self control
and forgiveness
But I believe I'll be okay
I'm okay with my broken brain

I'm happy with my silly body and love
my mismatch friends

We'll be okay.
Yeah, we'll be okay.

I took my meds this morning,
had therapy,
made some jam from scratch,
and continued creating art;
like I did the day before.
Life is very daunting.
But I have high hopes for myself.
I hope you do too.

So that is the end. Thank you for making it here.
And thank you for existing long enough to do so,
please continue doing that!
Take some time for yourself, a lot of these poems were very
emotional so please let yourself take a moment if you need
to.
It means absolutely everything to me that you've made it to
the end.
That you deemed my art good enough for your time. From
the deepest of my repairing heart, thank you.
That touches my soul. If you take anything away from this
please know, recovery isn't linear.
There is not a staircase going up and up.
Relapse is okay, and part of recovery.
Please stay safe and treat yourself how you would treat your
true love.
Manifest everything you desire and practise self praise.
I hope you truly love yourself as much as you should,
in the mean time we can work on it together!
You are *never* alone!

- from me to you

Some poetry describing some of my lowest lows
in hopes that speaking on such things will make more people aware that they're not in their battle alone.

It is okay to not be okay.
It is okay to not be okay.

Printed in Great Britain
by Amazon